INVOKE!

Calling God's Name
FOR
Faith and Action

Reed D. Tibbetts

INVOKE!
© 2016 by Reed D. Tibbetts

Published by Insight International, Inc.
contact@freshword.com
www.freshword.com
918-493-1718

All rights reserved. No part of this book may be reproduced or transmitted in any form or by any means, electronic or mechanical, including photocopying and recording, or by an information storage and retrieval system, without permission in writing from the author.

All Scripture quotations, unless otherwise noted, are taken from the *New American Standard Bible®*, © 1960, 1962, 1963, 1968, 1971, 1972, 1973, 1975, 1977, 1995 by The Lockman Foundation. Used by permission.www.Lockman.org

Scripture quotations marked "KJV" are taken from the King James Version of the Bible.

Scripture quotation marked "RSV" is taken from the *Revised Standard Version* of the Bible, copyright © 1952 [2nd edition, 1971] by the Division of Christian Education of the National Council of the Churches of Christ in the United States of America. Used by permission. All rights reserved.

Scripture quotation marked "ASV" is taken from the American Standard Version of the Bible.

ISBN: 978-1-943361-02-1
E-book ISBN: 978-1-943361-03-8

Library of Congress Control Number: 2015947519

Printed in the United States of America.

ENDORSEMENT FOR *INVOKE!*

"Reed serves faithfully and loyally as one of the elders in the church that I pastor. He is one of the best theological minds I have had the privilege of calling my friend. His teachings are a unique mix of potent ingredients that form a special recipe of the truth, and reach the minds and spirits of those he teaches. Relax, receive and enjoy the concepts of his latest book, *Invoke!*"

—Mike Connaway,
Senior Pastor of VLife Church,
McKinney, Texas

DEDICATION

I dedicate this book "INVOKE!" to my father in the Lord: Apostle Dick Benjamin. Dick was the founding pastor of Abbott Loop Christian Center in Anchorage, Alaska. I first came in contact with Dick in 1980, in Seattle, Washington. Dick had been ordained as an apostle, and as part of his vision of ministry, had sent out many, many people in teams to plant new churches throughout the United States. As a result of his counsel, I became part of one of those outreach churches: Southwest Seattle Christian Center. For my Bible College days, and the early years of my pastoral ministry, I had enjoyed the benefit of several fathers in the Lord, but no one of apostolic authority and doctrine. It was through his teaching that I was first exposed to the name of the Lord Jesus Christ as the new covenant name of God. Dick has always been a great teacher of the Word, with logic, context and authority. Dick's very simple principle of hermeneutics: **"Scripture interprets Scripture,"** has been my guide in accurately handling the word of truth. Over the next twenty years, my understanding and acceptance of the importance of God's Name in the life of every Christian developed; but it all started with my study of Dick's teachings on the topic. Dick is retired now, living in Anchorage. I still call him upon occasion, to talk over certain points of doctrine, and to ask for advice in my ministry, and he still gives apostolic advice, with humility and authority. Thank you, Dick, for laying down your life for the sake of the gospel, and inspiring me to be a guardian of apostolic doctrine. I love you, brother.

CONTENTS

Introduction 11

Chapter One   Traditions of Invoking 13
I come in the name of Caesar!
Open up, in the name of the Law!

Chapter Two   Invoke God's Name over
the Sons of Israel 17
So they shall put My Name on
the Sons of Israel, and I will bless them

Chapter Three   Invoke God's Name to
Heal the Land 21
If My people over whom My Name
is called will humble themselves

Chapter Four   For the Sake of the
Name Invoked 23
Thy Name is called upon us.
Do not forsake us!

Chapter Five   They Haven't Had God's
Name Invoked 27
Like those who haven't had
Thy Name called upon them

Chapter Six   Invoke God's Name to
Intimidate the People
of the Earth? 31
And they shall be afraid of you

Chapter Seven   What About God's Name
being Invoked on
the Gentiles? 35
God wants His Name called
upon all who accept Him

Chapter Eight	Hiding God's Formal Name..........39 *A definite practice of discouraging the speaking of the Name*	
Chapter Nine	The Magnified Name – Psalm 138:2..........45 *You have magnified Your word according to all Your name*	
Chapter Ten	Did the Patriarchs Know the Name?..........47 *But by My name, YHWH, I did not make Myself known to them*	
Chapter Eleven	So What is the Name?..........51 *Now they may say to me, 'What is His name?'*	
Chapter Twelve	God's Name Invoked on Christians at Baptism..........55 *Baptizing them in the Name of the Father and the Son and the Holy Spirit*	
Chapter Thirteen	Chart it Out: The Name at Water Baptism..........59 *Line things out in some kind of topical or chronological way*	
Chapter Fourteen	The Name Invoked in Circumcision..........63 *Every male among you shall be circumcised*	
Chapter Fifteen	The Ultimate Name in the End..........67 *What will every tongue confess?*	
Chapter Sixteen	No Jesus!..........71 *Remember: No Jesus in the prayer*	

Chapter Seventeen	When was the Name Invoked?................75 *Yahweh bless you and keep you*	
Chapter Eighteen	When Should We Invoke the Name?.................77 *When do you want God to swing into action?*	
Chapter Nineteen	Hallelujah................81 *Michael row the boat ashore*	
Chapter Twenty	Other Ways We May Practice Name Insignificance..............87 *Why limit your vocabulary in such a rude and crude way?*	
Chapter Twenty-One	Subjective Reflections.............93 *My brother, my nephew, my niece and my grand nephew*	
Chapter Twenty-Two	And More Subjective Reflections................97 *A daughter and a grandson*	
Chapter Twenty-Three	Boast the Name!...............103 *Some trust in chariots and some in horses*	
In Closing 107		

INTRODUCTION

Invoke! The word sounds like something strong, commanding and even mysterious. The dictionary gives several definitions: 1. to petition for help or support; 2. to appeal to or cite as authority; 3. to call forth by incantation: conjure; 4. to make an earnest request for: solicit; 5. to put into effect or operation: implement; 6. to bring about: cause. 21st century people don't use the word; it's almost archaic. The practice of invoking has a rich history in the Bible and throughout the church age, but it has slowly lost its meaning. It is still used, but rarely, and mostly in reference to some formal religious service, when the printed program or the master of ceremonies refers to the "Invocation." For most of us that means some kind of formal, fancy prayer to begin things. But what if God intended it to mean much more? What if there is something strong, something powerful, something commanding? What if it has become mysterious to us because we have lost track of something truly divine? What if we can unlock deeper dimensions of faith in our lives? Have we been missing something? Invoke!

Chapter One

TRADITIONS OF INVOKING

Throughout history humans have taken actions in the name of their gods or in the name of their leaders. They have willingly performed, spent, fought and even died in someone's name. We can picture hordes of Mongols charging into battle, while screaming the name of Genghis Khan, or huge masses of Celts crying out their leader's name as they ran into battle. As Christians we want to be successful soldiers in whatever battle our Lord wants us in. But what name are we calling out as we fight?

During the times of the Roman Empire, a person's task and mission could be guaranteed support and success, if they could say, "I come in the name of Caesar." To paraphrase what it meant: "Receive me, help me accomplish my mission, and send me on my way." Citizens and authorities throughout the empire would snap to and help out, for fear of punishment that would come from Caesar if they didn't! For the tasks and missions that we are moving forward to do as Christians, what name do we say we come in? Is it enough to say we are Christians? Here in the United States, people have almost been conditioned to disregard, or even have contempt for "Christians."

INVOKE!

We have heard invoking phrases or similar exclamations in old movies and TV westerns for years. The police would shout: "Open up in the name of the law" before they broke the door down. When chasing a suspect, they would shout: "Police! Stop!" Someone theorized that the phrase "Stop in the name of the law!" came into being in England when the first police force was formed by Sir Robert Peel, Home Secretary, in 1829. Initially it consisted of 1000 "Peelers" or "Bobbies" who maintained law and order in London. When approaching a suspected criminal, they could command them to stop by saying, "Stop! In the name of the law!" If the person tried to run off he would be chased by the police officer still shouting his "stop" order and blowing a warning whistle. This frequently encouraged members of the public to join in the chase and capture the suspect. The use of this phrase was to invoke the authority and power of the police force, for the suspect and the public to be aware of. What name or phrase should we be using to invoke authority and power, and even get cooperation in accomplishing great things for the Lord?

How much more should we who serve the living God practice invoking His Name to help us and bless our efforts?

Over the last two decades, we have become very aware of the millions of people worldwide who are Muslims. "Allah is his name, and Mohammed is his prophet." In these times, some Muslims invoke the name of Allah before doing whatever they are moving forward to do. Their motives may be different at times, but they are looking for God's help and blessing in the situation. And they are intense in doing this. How much

TRADITIONS OF INVOKING

more should we who serve the living God practice invoking His Name to help us and bless our efforts?

I once was hired as a General Manager for a pilot recycling project. I was hired long distance by two key upper managers in Connecticut and Georgia. The previous GM had been fired, and I was quickly hired because they had a building site that needed to be completed quickly for a formal grand opening. The very next day I had to visit the site and make sure things were on course. There were 2 employees, another Connecticut manager, and two contractors on site. When I arrived on location, they all looked at me strangely, as if to say, "Who the heck are you and what are you doing here?" One statement from me got everyone on track and moving forward. "I'm the new General Manager, and Larry and Bob sent me out here to make sure everything is on track as it should be." Everyone immediately filled me in and proceeded to do what they needed to do. All I had to do to be received by everyone and to get things moving forward was to invoke the right names. What do we need to be invoking in order to be received properly and to get things moving forward?

Fr. John Jay Hughes related that on a walk, many years ago, through an area in northern Germany, he came upon a shepherd, sitting on a rock, with his sheep grazing nearby. A dog was keeping the sheep together, occasionally bringing a sheep back that had wandered away from the flock. He asked the shepherd what the dog's name was. "I'll spell it for you," the shepherd replied. "I never say his name unless I want him to do something."

I see two simple truths in this little story. Firstly the shepherd only said the dog's name when he wanted him to do something. That's why we should be circumspect about invoking God's name: do it when you want Him to do something. Secondly

INVOKE!

the dog knew that when his name was spoken, he was going to be expected to do something. Now how much more does our Heavenly Father know that when we invoke His name, we are hoping for action on His part? And He is so ready to use His power on our behalf!

Chapter Two

INVOKE GOD'S NAME OVER THE SONS OF ISRAEL

Numbers 6:23-27 - Thus you shall bless the sons of Israel. You shall say to them: "The LORD bless you and keep you; the LORD make His face shine on you, and be gracious to you; the LORD lift up His countenance on you, and give you peace." So they shall invoke (put) My name on the sons of Israel, and I then will bless them.

This Scripture is referred to as the "Priestly Blessing". In it God does not specify when or how often they were to follow this command. But it stands to reason that if doing this would result in God blessing the people, the more often they did it, the better. In Temple times the tradition was for the priests to bless the people with this priestly blessing every morning after the sacrifices. Today many synagogues end their service with this blessing as their benediction. Members of individual households are blessed with this blessing on each Sabbath.

The Jewish people put a major emphasis on the exact wording of the blessing, and over the years, they developed and added a very specific and exact way of lifting their arms, using their hands, and extending their fingers. When recited, the priest raises his hands, palms facing outward and the thumbs of the outspread hands touching. The four fingers on each hand are split in the middle (you know, like the Vulcan hand sign accompanying the phrase, "Live long and prosper"). In this way the hands form the Hebrew letter Shin, an emblem for Shaddai. Thus it is done with exact words and exact motions. The attitude toward this blessing is very serious, positive and formal, almost like an ordination.

But the command had two parts: the blessing and the invoking. They ritualized and articulated the blessing, but what I consider to be the more important part of the command, putting God's name (Yahweh) on the sons of Israel, they did not emphasize. Often they will substitute Adonai (Lord) in place of Yahweh. They speak very little about "calling the Name." But they were very specific about the rest of the wording, they used Adonai in place of Yahweh, and they developed very careful ritual motions. At the least this shows inconsistent treatment of God's command, and at the most it is a crucial error.

Why would they do this? It has to do with their religious caution about pronouncing God's formal name out loud. Somehow they think that if they don't say the name, they won't violate the commandment: Thou shalt not take the name of Yahweh your God in vain.

> "Use these words to call My name on the people,
> and after you do that, I will bless them."

God makes it clear in the priestly blessing passage that they are to put God's name on, or call God's name over, the people.

INVOKE GOD'S NAME OVER THE SONS OF ISRAEL

God made it clear that they were to do that, and then He would bless them. He basically said, "Use these words to call My name on the people, and after you do that, I will bless them."

Perhaps the Jewish leaders thought they were the ones delivering the blessing (even today some religious leaders like to think they are the ones blessing God's people), but in truth God is the one who blesses; the religious leaders are the ones who are to put God's name on the people (or call God's name over the people). The key to releasing the blessing of God upon His people is to call His name, Yahweh, over them. Putting Yahweh's name on them, calls upon and releases God's volitional power, and He releases it in blessings, to honor His name.

What do I mean by releasing God's volitional power? God is all powerful and whatever He releases His power to accomplish gets done – period. But I want us to see something unique and deeper in this. We have emotions, intellect and volition (will). So does God. When we decide we're going to do something, we put the strength of our will, our volition, behind it. Because we are human, sometimes our effort is stronger, sometimes weaker, depending upon how strong we feel about swinging into action. God on the other hand, never chooses to do anything half way. When He chooses to do something, the full, 100% strength and power of His will is behind it, and it flat out gets done! God has told us that He will honor the invoking of His name with the full power and strength of His will – His volition. When we invoke God's name, He will release His volitional power and swing into action on our behalf! Now that's something!

Chapter Three

INVOKE GOD'S NAME TO HEAL THE LAND

II Chronicles 7:14 - and my people who are called by My name (literally – over whom My name is called) *humble themselves and pray, and seek My face, and turn from their wicked ways, then I will hear from heaven, will forgive their sin, and will heal their land.*

This passage is part of God's promise to Solomon, at the dedication of the Temple. Solomon's father David was a great warrior and king over Israel. Scripture records that he was a man after God's own heart (I Samuel 13:14; Acts 13:22). Even though we know that David abused his kingly power, committing adultery and murder, yet God loved him and blessed his line through all the generations to Jesus. At one point King David took note that he himself dwelled in a house of cedar, but the ark of God dwelled within a tent. He decided that He wanted to build a house for Yahweh.

I Chronicles 22:8 – But the word of the LORD came to me, saying, "You have shed much blood and have waged great wars; you shall not build a house to My name, because you have shed so much blood on the earth before Me. Behold, a son will be born to you, who shall be a man of rest; and I will give him rest from all his enemies on every side; for his name shall be Solomon, and I will give peace and quiet to Israel in his days. He shall build a house for My name, . . .

INVOKE!

So David made some of the preparations and gathered materials, but Solomon was the king who completed building the Temple in Jerusalem. It was a tremendous land mark in the history of Israel. All the people had gathered in Jerusalem to celebrate. Solomon offered a special Prayer of Dedication, and the Shekinah glory of God filled the temple. Solomon and the people offered 22,000 oxen and 120,000 sheep in sacrifice, as part of the dedication! The great feast lasted seven days, followed by a solemn assembly on the 8th day. The people returned to their tents; all in all a very happy and successful time. This was a big deal, people!

But it was based upon a crucial condition. What?

Then the LORD appeared to Solomon at night and promised His blessings for Solomon and all the people if they followed Him. He also cautioned Solomon to keep His statutes and ordinances, and to walk with Him just as David had. In the beginning of this extraordinary exhortation God stated that if He held back the rain, or sent the locusts to devour the land, or sent pestilence among the people, because of their wicked ways, that He would forgive their sin and heal their land. But it was based upon a crucial condition. What?

The people that God's name Yahweh had been called over needed to humble themselves, pray and seek God, and turn from their wicked ways. The pivotal point: that the people would turn around. The divine point: that God would act in their favor because His volitional power would be released since His name, Yahweh, had been called over them.

Chapter Four

FOR THE SAKE OF THE NAME INVOKED

Jeremiah 14:9 – Yet You are in our midst, O LORD, and we are called by Your name (literally – Your name is called upon us). *Do not forsake us.*

Daniel 9:18, 19 - O LORD hear! O LORD forgive! O LORD listen and take action! For Your own sake, O my God, do not delay, because Your city and Your people are called by Your name (literally – have Your name called upon them).

II Chronicles 36:20,21 – Those who had escaped from the sword, he (Nebuchadnezzar) carried away to Babylon; and they were servants to him and to his sons until the rule of the kingdom of Persia, to fulfill the word of the LORD by the mouth of Jeremiah, until the land had enjoyed its Sabbaths. All the days of its desolation it kept Sabbath until seventy years were complete.

Jeremiah 29:10 – For thus says the LORD, When seventy years have been completed for Babylon, I will visit you and fulfill My good word to you, to bring you back to this place.

The prophets did not hesitate to call upon God for help and restoration for the sake of His name that had been called upon the people. It meant something to them that God's name had been called upon His people many years ago, and was called upon them now; and they sincerely believed that it meant something to Him.

> **Finally God pronounced judgment upon them, and it took the form of destruction and captivity.**

Through its long history, the nation of Israel just wouldn't serve God consistently. When there was a righteous king, the people would return to Yahweh, but when an evil king would come to power, the people would turn away from Yahweh, and worship other gods. Even when they followed all the feasts and sacrifices to Yahweh, they didn't follow Him from the heart. Finally God pronounced judgment upon them, and it took the form of destruction and captivity. The final king of Israel was Zedekiah, a puppet king, put in place by Nebuchadnezzar. He did evil in God's sight; he wouldn't listen to Jeremiah, the prophet of God. He actually tried to rebel against Nebuchadnezzar. The armies of Babylon were sent against Israel. It was a slaughter, with the young and old, men and women, sickly and well, slain with the sword. All the treasures and possessions in the temple of Yahweh and the palace of the king were taken back to Babylon. The temple of Yahweh was burned and the walls of Jerusalem were pulled down. The people who had not been killed were enslaved and taken back to Babylon. We know about some of the royalty that were taken away: Shadrach, Meshach, Abednego, Daniel. We have all been told the Sunday School stories. Even though things had gone very badly for the people of Israel, some still held firm to their belief in Yahweh. God honored that faithfulness with miracles of protection. After many years in Babylon, Daniel was reading the Scripture and found in the book of Jeremiah that the desolation of Jerusalem was completed after 70 years, and it was now the time that God said he would restore Jerusalem.

Since God's Word promised the restoration, he could have simply spoke it out loud to everyone. He could have declared the truth, confessed the restoration and sat back and watched God's hand move (you know, confess and possess). But that's not what happened. Daniel went into a serious time of prayer, humbling himself, repenting, and asking for God's forgiveness. And then he appealed for volitional power and action from God because the name of God (Yahweh) had been called upon the people of Israel and upon the city of Jerusalem. He didn't tell God that he had to do it because of His Word. But He understood the importance of the invoked name of God, and he understood the volitional power contained in the invoking of the name of Yahweh upon His people and upon Jerusalem. So He appealed to that invocation, and that is what Yahweh honored!

Chapter Five

THEY HAVEN'T HAD GOD'S NAME INVOKED

Isaiah 63:19 - We have become like those over whom You have never ruled, like those who were not called by Your name (literally haven't had Your name called upon them).

The Israelites knew that they were God's special people. During the times when they drifted away from following the Law of Moses, when they worshipped other gods, they still considered themselves a special people because God had chosen them and His name, Yahweh, had been called over them. They knew that God honored His name and responded to His people who were called by His name. Even when they did not honor Him, they expected special treatment because of His name over them. That doesn't make sense, but they still had a cocky kind of pride and false sense of protection.

When we come to Isaiah 63, the circumstance and thoughts of the Israelites are recorded, when because of their disobedience and rebellion, God's anger and wrath had been loosed upon them. It had come to the point where they were defeated and destroyed. As they reflected upon their past history, remembering how God had taken care of them under the leadership of Moses, they were asking, "Where is the God of old?" And they came to the shocking realization that they were being treated as though Yahweh had never been their ruler, and His name had never been called upon them! Talk about a reality check!

> **And they came to the shocking realization that they were being treated as though Yahweh had never been their ruler, and His name had never been called upon them!**

Now please understand. Our God is not a vengeful God, just waiting for us to fall short, so He can punish us. Quite to the contrary, God is not willing that any should perish, but that all would come to repentance. Repentance . . . is the practice of realizing that when the actions you are taking and the direction you are heading are wrong; so you are to stop, turn around, and head in the right direction. Even with His people in the Old Testament, God was so concerned that they turn around and head in the right direction, that He willingly withdrew His blessing, until they could be shocked into turning again to the Lord.

God's loving-kindness, longsuffering and mercy went a long way in overlooking sin and rebellion in His people. After all, His name had been called over them, and He honored that a long time. But when they presumed upon that, and sinned all the more, it didn't work forever. That is also true for us today. Our Lord Jesus Christ loves us, forgives us and doesn't remember our sin against us. But He does not want us to presume upon His mercy. As Paul stated in Romans 6, "Are we to continue in sin so that grace may increase? May it never be!" Shall we sin because we are not under law but under grace? May it never be!" Where sin increased, grace abounded all the more, and we are covered by the grace of our Lord Jesus Christ. But let's not set up our camp site on the grounds of sin. Instead, let's possess the abundant life, the life of grace and righteousness that the people that have His name called over them should possess.

Lord Jesus Christ, I will not be presumptuous. I call your name over every aspect of my life, and I will live in grace, righteousness and abundance for You!

Chapter Six

INVOKE GOD'S NAME TO INTIMIDATE THE PEOPLE OF THE EARTH?

Deuteronomy 28:10 - So all the peoples of the earth will see that you are called by the name of the LORD (literally shall see that the name of the LORD is called upon you), *and they shall be afraid of you.*

It was a tremendous gathering when the Israelites assembled on Mt. Gerizim and Mt. Ebal, after they had taken the Promised Land. Half of the tribes were on one mountain and half were on the other. Curses were pronounced from Mt. Ebal and blessings from Mt. Gerizim. It all had to do with whether or not the people would keep the commandments of Yahweh and walk in His ways. We're looking at the part where fantastic results and blessings would come to them as they kept the commandments and walked in His ways. God points out in verse 10 that all the people in the world who saw these fantastic results and blessings would realize that the Israelites had the name of Yahweh called upon them, and they would fear them.

Now being feared was a good thing, in the sense that other peoples and nations would hesitate to attack them, for fear of God's opposition to them. So having the name of Yahweh called upon them did produce a positive result in intimidating all the other peoples of the earth. But I also see a tremendous evangelistic element to this. God was saying that all the other peoples of the earth would see the fantastic results and blessings that the Israelites had, as they kept the commandments of Yahweh and walked in His ways. And they would want Yahweh to be their God. The same is true for us today. We want the name of the Lord Jesus Christ called over every aspect of our lives, and we want to walk in His ways, and enjoy the blessings and abundance that He has for us. That will be a tremendous testimony to all the people around us. They will want to have the Lord in their lives, and to live in His ways. Old Testament prophecy indicates that in the end times, all the people of the earth will want to be taught the ways of Yahweh, so that they can walk in them. And the prophecies indicate that they will come to Mt. Zion (an Old Testament type of the church) to be taught His ways so they can walk in His paths. They will want to have the name of the Lord Jesus Christ called over their lives too! That sounds like a great way to bring people to Jesus, doesn't it?

> **They will want to have the Lord in their lives, and to live in His ways.**

Just one more thought. It seems to me that in the United States it has become unpopular to be called a Christian, or to be identified as a Christian organization. Anti-Christian groups and some in the media show contempt and disregard for anything Christian. And the general public sees the Christian church as a powerless, archaic organization. The time is now here for us to counteract this false impression. We need to be the people who show forth the power of God, and the wonder working power that is in His name. Followers of the Lord Jesus Christ, arise, and invoke His name, so that all the peoples of the earth will see what He has done and be afraid of opposing Him or His people! More important than that, the peoples of the earth will want to be His people and have the name of the Lord Jesus Christ called over them. This is the pure evangelism that God wants to see happen so that all will come to Him in repentance and faith.

Chapter Seven

WHAT ABOUT GOD'S NAME BEING INVOKED ON THE GENTILES?

Amos 9:11,12 – In that day I will raise up the fallen booth of David, and wall up its breaches; I will also raise up its ruins and rebuild it as in the days of old; that they may possess the remnant of Edom and all the nations who are called by My name (literally over whom My name has been called).

Acts 15:14-18 – Simeon has related how God first concerned Himself about taking from among the Gentiles a people for His name. With this the words of the Prophets agree, just as it is written, "After these things I will return, and I will rebuild the tabernacle of David which has fallen, And I will rebuild its ruins, and I will restore it, so that the rest of mankind may seek the LORD, and all the Gentiles who are called by My name (literally over whom My name is called)," *says the LORD who makes these things known from long ago.*

The early church was composed almost entirely of Jewish people, but as we know God wanted the gospel of the Lord Jesus Christ taken to all mankind. Peter had to have special visions and divine appointments to convince him of that. Paul had to have the Damascus road visitation, to bring him to Christ. He was told by Christ to go to the Gentiles, and so he embraced his mission and went for it in a big way. But some of the Jewish Christians, especially Pharisees who were Christians, believed that Gentiles could become Christians, but they would also have to be circumcised and observe the law of Moses. In other words they would have to become proselytes of the Jewish religion. This was a very divisive issue and so we see the first Church Council occur, in Jerusalem, to resolve this issue. It was resolved correctly, and salvation through grace by faith in the Lord Jesus Christ was set forth for the Gentiles, without the addition of Old Covenant Jewish law.

> **James did not hesitate to note that the practice of God's name being called over His people should continue.**

In the midst of all this discussion and speech making, we see the final summation by James, the head of the church in Jerusalem. In that summation he refers to the calling of God's name over people. This concept was well understood by the Jews, as they had God's name, Yahweh, called over them. In referring to the Gentiles becoming followers of the Lord Jesus Christ, James saw the identical concept for members of the Church: that God's covenant name would be called over them. At this major point in time, where they did not want to lay undue burdens and practices upon the Gentile Christians, James did not hesitate to note that the practice of God's name being called over His people should continue. And this also shows God's evangelistic heart, in that in Old Covenant times, all non-Jewish people could come to Him

WHAT ABOUT GOD'S NAME BEING INVOKED ON THE GENTILES?

through the proselyte process. And in New Covenant times His name would be called over all Christian people, Jewish and non-Jewish. God wants His name called over everyone who accepts Him: the Lord Jesus Christ wants His name called over everyone who accepts Him. By making this declaration, James clearly shows that the calling of God's name over His people is a crucial concept, practice and doctrine that carries through the Old Covenant and into the New Covenant.

Chapter Eight

HIDING GOD'S FORMAL NAME

Over the centuries, it has been said by some that the Jewish people have tried to hide God's formal name from non-Jewish people. Have they really tried to hide the name of Yahweh from the rest of us?

The name "Yahweh" occurs 6,828 times in the Scripture. That alone should tell us that God wanted His name known and used. He wanted His name called over His people frequently; hence he instructed that it was to be repeated three times in the priestly blessing (the blessing that was pronounced daily in the Temple).

The Jewish people took the 3rd commandment very seriously. "You shall not take the name of the LORD (Yahweh) your God in vain, for the LORD (Yahweh) will not leave him unpunished who takes His name in vain." (Exodus 20:7). God's intent in the commandment was that His people regard His name with reverence and respect, and not to invoke it in disrespectful or frivolous ways. Over the years the Jewish people took that further. For fear that they might not be as respectful as they should, they stopped saying or writing the Name, and substituted another word (Adonai) for it.

INVOKE!

> **At the time of the Babylonian captivity Jewish rabbinical law became very strict in the belief that the Name of God was far too sacred to speak.**

At the time of the Babylonian captivity Jewish rabbinical law became very strict in the belief that the Name of God was far too sacred to speak, except by the priesthood, and by them only in secret study or on special days. This is shown in the Mishnah (Sanhedrin 10:1), and the Talmud further comments on this passage, saying that many rabbis taught that whoever is speaking the Name outside of these restrictions would forfeit any right to the afterlife, and should be put to death.

The Jewish historian, Josephus (AD 37-100) wrote about Moses, saying, "Whereupon God declared to him his holy name, which had never been discovered to men before; concerning which it is not lawful for me to say any more (Antiquities of the Jews – Book II, Chapter 12, par. 4). Josephus had been taught by the Pharisees not to pronounce God's proper name – not even to write it.

Philo (20 BC-AD 50), commenting on the life of Moses, wrote: "But if any one were, I will not say to blaspheme against the Lord of gods and men, but were even to dare to utter his name unseasonably, he must endure the punishment of death;" Philo went on to express the idea that we do not call our parents by their given names, but instead use "Mother" or "Father" out of respect. So too, we should not use God's formal name, since it is most holy and divine. To keep from

HIDING GOD'S FORMAL NAME

using God's formal name too freely or carelessly, we should not use it, speak it or write it.

The Jewish people held the name of God in deep reverence, and as a practice, did not pronounce it. When making copies of the Scripture, the scribe would transcribe the name, Yahweh, but was instructed not to pronounce it. Instead he was to utter a less sacred name, such as Adonai or Elohim. That way the listener wouldn't hear "Yahweh" pronounced. The Masorites were Hebrew scribes during the Middle Ages, who would write the name Yahweh, but the vowel marks that they put into the Name were from the Hebrew words Elohim or Adonai. This was probably to prevent the correct pronouncing of Yahweh. According to Unger's Bible Dictionary, the Jews, out of a superstitious reverence, always, in reading the Scripture, would substitute Adonai for Yahweh.

It has been said that the Jewish scholars who worked on the Septuagint (Greek translation of the Pentateuch) substituted the word Adonai wherever they found the word Yahweh, but that was not true. It was actually Christian scholars who instituted that practice, and we're not sure why they did it: could it be that they took on the Jewish approach of hiding the Name so it would not be pronounced?

According to the Jewish set of rules and practices (Halakha), secondary rules are to be set around a primary law, in order to reduce the chance that the main law will be broken. To keep from taking the name "Yahweh" in vain, or blaspheming it, practices were instituted to guard against the pronouncing of God's proper name. These secondary rules would keep the Name from being repeated carelessly, or uttered unseasonably.

On a personal note, I remember a telephone conversation I had back in 1981. At the time I was studying God's Name throughout the Scriptures, in preparation for sermons I would be preaching in a local church in Seattle. I had several questions about Old Testament Scriptures that made statements about Yahweh. I called a rabbi in the local Jewish congregation to ask him specific questions about God's name being used in certain Jewish ceremonies. It was a very unusual call; the rabbi did not know me, and I kept asking very specific questions about the use of God's name. He seemed to deflect every question I asked. It was taking far longer than I had planned, and I was growing impatient with the conversation. Suddenly it dawned on me that I was putting this spiritual leader in a very bad position. As a Jewish leader he had been trained in the reverent and careful use of God's name, and now some Protestant Christian pastor was putting him on the spot, asking about pronunciation and use of God's formal name! I apologized for my "pressing" approach in the conversation, thanked him for his help, and hung up. What a way for me to treat a man who was simply honoring his reverential respect for the name of God.

But out of reverence and respect they developed practices that definitely discouraged the speaking of God's name.

What I have come to realize is that Jewish people were not attempting to hide the name of Yahweh with all of these practices, rules and secondary rules. But out of reverence and respect they developed practices that definitely discouraged the speaking of God's name. It does show that the Jewish people believed this name, Yahweh, was special, and required more reverence than other names or titles.

HIDING GOD'S FORMAL NAME

But is it possible that these restrictive ideas have resulted in God's Name not being called over His people, when it could have been releasing God's volitional power? We cry out for more power from God, but is it possible that our cautious reverence sometimes robs us of experiencing God's powerful blessing?

Chapter Nine

THE MAGNIFIED NAME - PSALM 138:2

KJV - I will worship toward thy holy temple, and praise thy name for thy lovingkindness and for thy truth: for thou hast magnified thy word above thy entire name.

RSV - I bow down toward thy holy temple and give thanks to thy name for thy steadfast love and thy faithfulness; for thou hast exalted above everything thy name and thy word.

NASB - Psalm 138:2 I will bow down toward Your holy temple and give thanks to Your name for Your lovingkindness and Your truth; for you have magnified Your word according to all Your name.

It's no accident that God teaches us to value His word highly. And it's obvious that God places a high value on His Name.

Years ago while I was attending Bible College, we used to sit around in Systematic Theology class and afterward in the Student Union Building, and discuss/debate unusual Bible topics. We were full of ourselves and full of opinions, and a lot of it seems ridiculous now, as I look back 40 years. One discussion that I remember was about Psalm 138:2. The big question was what God viewed as higher (more important): His name or His word? I was amazed at how strong the competing opinions were. God's Word is the most important! God's Name is the most important! Since I hadn't studied anything about God's Name, I just assumed His word was more important. Based on the King James Version, His word was above His name. But the argument was put forward that the Hebrew scholars who worked on the Greek Septuagint version altered the wording somewhat, so that God's name would be de-emphasized, and non-Jewish people wouldn't pay attention to God's name (there is no good evidence that they ever did this). Supposedly it was part of a conspiracy to keep the special name of God hidden from non-Jews. I have always liked a good mystery, so I looked at some of the more modern versions, which were based upon additional manuscripts that had been found in the years since 1611, when the King James Version had been published. I knew a little bit of Hebrew, since I had one quarter of Biblical Hebrew, so I stumbled through the Hebrew text to try and sort it out. The best translation that I could come up with was this: "You have exalted Your Word together with and according to Your Name." What it showed me is that the argument over whether His Word or His Name were more important was ridiculous, but that the name of God and the word of God are both very important. It's taken me a lot of years and exposure to a lot of good Bible teaching to understand this concept intertwining the importance of God's Word and His Name. It's no accident that God teaches us to value His word highly. And it's obvious that God places a high value on His Name. We may get sidetracked with foolish disputes and speculations, but He wants us to know and practice the power of His Name.

Chapter Ten

DID THE PATRIARCHS KNOW THE NAME?

Exodus 6:2,3 – God spoke further to Moses and said to him, "I am the LORD (YHWH); *and I appeared to Abraham, Isaac, and Jacob, as God Almighty,* **but by My name, LORD (YHWH),** *I did not make Myself known to them."*

God had appeared and made Himself known to the patriarchs as God Almighty (El Shaddai), but not as LORD (Yahweh). Was God saying that they didn't know the name Yahweh?

Genesis 4:26 – To Seth, to him also a son was born; and he called his name Enosh. Then men began to call upon the name of the LORD (YHWH)

Genesis 17:1 – Now when Abram was ninety-nine years old, the LORD (YHWH) *appeared to Abram and said to him, "I am God Almighty; walk before Me, and be blameless."*

Genesis 26:24 – (Isaac at Beersheba). The LORD (YHWH) *appeared to him the same night and said, "I am the God of your father Abraham; . . .*

Genesis 28:13 – (when Jacob had the dream of the ladder up to heaven, with angels ascending and descending on it). And behold, the LORD

INVOKE!

(YHWH) *stood above it and said, "I am the LORD* (YHWH), *the God of your father Abraham and the God of Isaac;* . . .

It looks like an error in Scripture.

To Abram God declared that He was God Almighty (El Shaddai). But in reality God's people (and that includes the patriarchs) did know the name YHWH. Men began to call on the name of YHWH (Gen. 4:26) long before the patriarchs. God actually spoke His name, YHWH to Jacob (Gen. 28:13). So what is this declaration that God made to Moses in Exodus 6:2, 3? It looks like an error in Scripture. What is the explanation? The answer to this seeming contradiction lies in understanding what God was saying about making Himself known by the name YHWH. While men did know God's name YHWH prior to Moses, they didn't really know the YHWH nature of God: the timeless eternity of God. They knew God's nature in the sense of power and might – God Almighty (El Shaddai).

Exodus 6:2,3 – God spoke further to Moses and said to him, "I am the LORD (YHWH); *and I appeared to Abraham, Isaac, and Jacob, as God Almighty (El Shaddai),* (showing my mighty and powerful nature), *but by My name, LORD* (YHWH), (and my timeless eternal nature), *I did not make Myself known to them."*

Humans all around the Israelites, in the time of Moses, had many gods, and depending upon their circumstances, gods came and went. The Egyptians and the people of the Middle East that would interact with God's people dropped old gods and picked up new gods regularly, depending upon the posi-

DID THE PATRIARCHS KNOW THE NAME?

tive developments in their circumstances. God knew that from Moses on, His people needed to have only one God, YHWH. YHWH is timeless and eternal – He would not come and go, but would be their one God forever. God needed to shake His people loose from the practice of all the people around them, who shifted their allegiance from one god to another, every time circumstances went badly. Or even worse, people would give honor to many gods, just to cover their bases. And so God laid it out in the first of the Ten Commandments: "I am Yahweh your God, who brought you out of the land of Egypt, out of the house of slavery. You shall have no other gods before Me."

> **God knew that from Moses on,
> His people needed to have only one God, YHWH.
> YHWH is timeless and eternal.**

Chapter Eleven

SO WHAT IS THE NAME?

God – Elohim Lord – Adonai LORD – YHWH
Lord GOD – Adonai YHWH

As we follow people in the Old Testament, we find that they used the term, "Elohim" in the same way we use the term God. In a more personal way, they would refer to God as "Adonai" like we use the term Lord. In more formal ways they referred to God as "Adonai YHWH," translated Lord GOD; or as "YHWH," translated LORD. Note that in most English translations of the Bible, GOD and LORD are all capital letters. That is the editors' way of showing the Hebrew word is God's formal name: YHWH. In the Old Testament, every time you see "LORD" or "GOD," it means that the Hebrew name "YHWH" was used.

Exodus 3:13 – Then Moses said to God, "Behold, I am going to the sons of Israel, and I will say to them, 'The God of your fathers has sent me to you.' Now they may say to me, 'What is His name?' What shall I say to them?"

Exodus 3:14 – God said to Moses, "I AM WHO I AM"; and He said, "Thus you shall say to the sons of Israel, 'I AM has sent me to you.'"

INVOKE!

Exodus 3:15 – God, furthermore, said to Moses, "Thus you shall say to the sons of Israel, 'The LORD (YHWH) the God of your fathers, the God of Abraham, the God of Isaac, and the God of Jacob, has sent me to you.' This is My name forever, and this is My memorial–name to all generations."

The exact pronunciation is not certain; perhaps it is pronounced Yahweh, or maybe Yahovah.

This is a distinct pivotal point in time for the Israelites. God is calling Moses to lead them out of Egypt and into the Promised Land. Moses asks God to tell him His name, so that He can communicate it to the Israelites. In that day and time, men worshipped all kinds of gods with different names. God responds "I AM WHO I AM." Tell them, "I AM (YHWH) has sent me to you." This is derived from the Hebrew term, "HAYAH", meaning "to be". It has a timeless sense, so you could say, "I was, I am, I will be," all wrapped into the one term. That's still too simple of an explanation. The word really expresses all forms of the verb, to be: is, was, being, will be, about to be, causing to be. It's all contained in this word. YHWH is referred to as the tetragrammaton, because it has four letters. The exact pronunciation is not certain; perhaps it is pronounced Yahweh, or maybe Yahovah. I've looked long and hard at the pronunciation possibilities, and have concluded that I don't know for sure. For the purposes of this book, I will use Yahweh. So God tells Moses it is His name forever, and His memorial-name to all generations. That should settle it: God's name is Yahweh. While many terms were used to refer to God in the Old Testament (under the

SO WHAT IS THE NAME?

Old Covenant) it is clear that God's formal name is Yahweh. The Israelites consider it God's formal name, God's sacred name and the national name of God for them.

Yet as we look in the New Testament at His disciples, and follow the early church we find no evidence that they called God by the name Yahweh. Even though they were born and raised as Jews, and trained to reverence the name of God, Yahweh, yet they didn't use it once in their sermons or epistles, as they established the church of Jesus Christ. We do have the use of the word "hallelujah" four times in Revelation chapter 19. It uses "Yah," the abbreviated form of Yahweh, and is a command to praise Yahweh. The four living creatures, the twenty-four elders and a great multitude in heaven command everyone to praise God, for Babylon, the great harlot has been thrown down, and it's time for the marriage supper of the Lamb! This end time reference is the only New Testament use of the name Yahweh. Or is it?

John 8:58, 59 – Jesus said to them, "Truly, truly, I say to you, before Abraham was born, I am. Therefore they took up stones to throw at Him, but Jesus hid Himself and went out of the temple.

Why do they take up stones to throw at Him?

This is such a compelling statement that Jesus made to the Jews in the temple. He says of Himself, "I am." Why do they take up stones to throw at Him? It is because they understood Him to be saying that He was God, and using God's memorial-name to refer to Himself. If they didn't believe He was God, then that was blasphemy, and He should be stoned to death for that. It was clear to them, and it should be clear to us. Jesus was saying, "I am Yahweh."

Matthew 1:21 – and you shall call his name Jesus; . . .

Luke 2:11 – for today in the city of David there has been born for you a Savior, who is Christ the Lord.

When the angels declared the birth of Jesus, they did not say His name was Yahweh. Jesus Christ the Lord is how they referred to Him.

John 17:11, 12. I am no longer in the world; and yet they themselves are in the world, and I come to You. Holy Father, keep them in Your name, the name which you have given Me, that they may be one even as We are. While I was with them, I was keeping them in Your name which you have given Me; and I guarded them and not one of them perished but the son of perdition, so that the Scripture would be fulfilled.

On the final night before He was arrested, tried and crucified, Jesus spoke many profound truths to His 11 disciples. Here in a prayer He expressed for them, He clearly states that God the Father had given His name to God the Son, and in that Name Jesus had guarded them, and that now and going forward, they would be kept (guarded, protected) in that Name. That name is the Lord Jesus Christ.

A lot has been made of God's name used in water baptism through the twentieth century. Let's follow the ordinance of water baptism through the New Testament Scriptures, and see what it can teach us about the New Covenant Name of God.

Chapter Twelve

GOD'S NAME INVOKED ON CHRISTIANS AT BAPTISM

James 2:7 (Apostle James) - Do they not blaspheme the fair name by which you have been called (which has been called upon you) (commentators: that is, at water baptism).

In James 2:1-7 we are provided good instruction in relating to the church. God wants to be sure that we do not show favoritism to rich people, while we dishonor the poor. He points out that the rich oppress people and drag them into court, and even blaspheme the name of the Lord Jesus Christ. Years ago when I was reading this passage and then looking over some commentaries for deeper understanding, one of the commentators addressed verse seven, saying that the literal Greek was referring to the fair name that was called upon the people, that is, at water baptism. This was the first time I had encountered this concept of the name being called upon Christians. In the Old Testament there were a number of references to God's name being called over or put on the Israelites, but this is the only use of exact language that called the name on Christians. As I looked further in other reference books, I found that this idea of the fair name being called upon Christians at water baptism was mentioned several times.

INVOKE!

Many commentators connected the calling of the name in this verse to what happens at water baptism, even though it is not mentioned specifically in the verse. They got the idea from understood practices in the early church.

That got me thinking about God's name at water baptism. What does the Scripture say?

Matthew 28:19,20 – the resurrected Jesus told his followers, *"Go therefore and make disciples of all the nations, baptizing them in the name of the Father and the Son and the Holy Spirit, teaching them to observe all that I commanded you; and lo, I am with you always, even to the end of the age."*

So what name did His followers call over the new disciples as they were being baptized in water?

Jesus clearly commanded His followers to baptize new disciples in the name. . . but the Father and the Son and the Holy Spirit, while clearly referring to the God-head (the Trinity), is not a name. So what name did His followers call over the new disciples as they were being baptized in water?

Acts 2:38 – *Repent, and each of you be baptized in the name of Jesus Christ for the forgiveness of your sins; . . .*

This was Peter speaking on the Day of Pentecost when 3,000 came to the Lord.

Acts 8:16 – *For He had not yet fallen upon any of them; they had simply been baptized in the name of the Lord Jesus.*

GOD'S NAME INVOKED ON CHRISTIANS AT BAPTISM

Philip had gone to Samaria and preached the gospel. Many were saved and baptized in water; then the apostles Peter and John were sent from Jerusalem to Samaria, so that they also would receive the Holy Spirit.

Acts 10:48 – And he ordered them to be baptized in the name of Jesus Christ.

In the house of Cornelius, as Peter was preaching, the Holy Spirit fell on those who were listening. They were saved, and Peter then commanded them to be baptized in water.

Acts 19:5 – When they heard this, they were baptized in the name of the Lord Jesus.

Paul was instructing some disciples in Ephesus in the correct water baptism. They had been baptized in the baptism of John the Baptist. So they got baptized again in the name of the Lord Jesus; then the Holy Spirit came upon them.

Romans 6:3 – Or do you not know that all of us who have been baptized into Christ Jesus have been baptized into His death?

Paul is explaining the meaning of water baptism: identifying with our Lord Jesus Christ in His death, burial and resurrection.

Galatians 3:27 – For all of you who were baptized into Christ have clothed yourself with Christ.

Paul is making it clear that all Jews and Gentiles who were baptized into Christ are all sons of God together.

Colossians 2:6, 12 - Having been buried with Him in baptism, in which you were also raised up with Him through faith in the working of God, who raised Him from the dead.

Instructing again, Paul emphasizes our identity with the Lord Jesus Christ. The "Him" of this verse refers back to verse six, where he says they have received Christ Jesus the Lord.

James 2:7 – Do they not blaspheme the fair name by which you have been called?

In the context verse one tells us what the fair name is: *"My brethren, do not hold your faith in our glorious Lord Jesus Christ with an attitude of personal favoritism."* It is God's desire that we treat all people equally, and avoid personal preferences in how we relate to others. He does not want the practice of our faith to be influenced by our personal preferences or prejudices.

I looked over these references to see how they lined up.

Chapter Thirteen

CHART IT OUT: THE NAME AT WATER BAPTISM

It always helps me to line things out in some kind of topical or chronological way (Maybe I'm a linear thinker). With these baptism references this is how they line up and chart out:

Matt. 28:19,20	**the Father**	**the Son**	**the Holy Spirit**
Acts 2:28		Jesus	Christ
Acts 8:16	Lord	Jesus	
Acts 10:48		Jesus	Christ
Acts 19:5	Lord	Jesus	
Rom. 6:3		Jesus	Christ
Gal. 3:27			Christ
Col. 2:6,12	Lord	Jesus	Christ
James 2:1,7	Lord	Jesus	Christ
	Lord	**Jesus**	**Christ**

Jesus commanded His followers to baptize in the name of the Father and the Son and the Holy Spirit. That exact phrase in reference to water baptism is not mentioned again. But the name of Jesus Christ is, as well as the name of the Lord Jesus, and the Lord Jesus Christ. This brings me to the conclusion that the name of the Father and the Son and the Holy Spirit is the Lord Jesus Christ. I believe that the triune name of our triune God, the name of the Father and the Son and the Holy Spirit is the LORD JESUS CHRIST. Within that triune name I believe that LORD reminds us of the Father, JESUS reminds us of the Son, and CHRIST reminds us of the Holy Spirit.

> **Jesus commanded His followers to baptize in the name of the Father and the Son and the Holy Spirit. That exact phrase in reference to water baptism is not mentioned again.**

If this is true, why didn't the Apostle Paul just write this down, exactly, in one of his epistles? I don't have an answer to that, but there were many things for the Christians in the first century church that were obvious and evident, while for us we have to pull together many verses and let Scripture interpret Scripture. That is what I have done here.

Jesus made very clear statements that His Father's name was the same name that the Father had given Him (John 17:11, 12). Father keep them in Your name, the name which you have given Me. As I look at all these Scriptures I can see that God the Son, the Lord Jesus Christ did have the New Covenant name of God, and He wanted His name called over every Christian who was baptized in water.

So when I baptize Christians, I like to say something like this: "Because you have confessed your faith in Jesus Christ, I now baptize you in the name of the Father and the Son and the

CHART IT OUT: THE NAME AT WATER BAPTISM

Holy Spirit – the Lord Jesus Christ." In saying this at water baptism, I am not simply expressing a preference; I believe this event in a Christian's life is so important that I want to call the new covenant name of God over the person being baptized, and embrace the releasing of His volitional power. And God wants His name called over the individual Christian at water baptism, and He will swing into action on their behalf!

Chapter Fourteen

THE NAME INVOKED IN CIRCUMCISION

In Old Testament times, circumcision was the physical sign of the Covenant between the Israelites and God. In New Testament times, water baptism is the physical sign of the Covenant between Christians and God. When I saw the emphasis on God's name being called over people being baptized, it made me wonder about God's name and Old Covenant circumcision.

Genesis 17:10-12 – Yahweh said to Abraham: *This is My covenant, which you shall keep, between Me and you and your descendants after you: every male among you shall be circumcised. And you shall be circumcised in the flesh of your foreskin, and it shall be the sign of the covenant between Me and you. And every male among you who is eight days old shall be circumcised throughout your generations, . . .*

First established in the Abrahamic Covenant and continued through the Mosaic Covenant (Old Covenant), the sign of the Old Covenant was the circumcision of every male.

Colossians 2:9-12 – *For in Him all the fullness of Deity dwells in bodily form, and in Him you have been made complete, and He is the head over all rule and authority; and in Him you were also circumcised with a circumcision made without hands, in the removal of the body of the flesh by the circumcision of Christ; having been buried with Him in baptism, in which you were also raised up with Him through faith in the working of God, who raised Him from the dead.*

But in the eyes of the non-Christian community around this person, it is not until he is baptized in water that it is accepted that he has become a Christian.

It has been taught and well accepted that water baptism is the sign of our New Covenant with the Lord Jesus Christ. When we are baptized in water it is an outward sign to the world that we are Christians. In more than one culture overseas, when a person accepts Jesus Christ as his Savior, he is a Christian in God's eyes. But in the eyes of the non-Christian community around this person, it is not until he is baptized in water that it is accepted that he has become a Christian. At that point the non-Christian family or community often rejects him and may even ostracize him.

So I have taught for a number of years that one of the special meanings of water baptism is that it is the action we take as an external sign that we are partakers of the New Covenant in the Lord Jesus Christ. It is the sign of the New Covenant.

That being said, I find it interesting that the first time that God's name is called over the Jewish male is at circumcision. There is no Scripture that states this specifically, but I have found this to be true, through research on the Jewish custom of circumcision. Let's take a look.

Brit milah means "covenant of circumcision." It is the Jewish ritual performed on the baby boy eight days after he is born, in

THE NAME INVOKED IN CIRCUMCISION

which the foreskin is removed from the penis by a mohel (person who is trained to safely perform the procedure). It is also known by the Yiddish word "bris." There is a formal ceremony involving the family and friends. Without going into the exact steps of the ceremony, there are two distinct times that a blessing is given. One blessing is pronounced by the mohel before the act of circumcision, and another is offered by the father afterward. The wording is almost identical and includes: "Blessed are You, Lord our God." The formal name of God, Yahweh, is used. In modern times, they do not pronounce the formal name of God, but instead substitute the term "Adonai." That is because the tradition has evolved to avoid pronouncing the formal name of God, to avoid using it in vain. But I do think that in times past they used the formal name of God without hesitation. So the first time God's name is pronounced and called over the new baby is at circumcision; at the performing of the sign of the Old Covenant.

The pattern continues in the New Covenant. God's name is pronounced and called over the new Christian at water baptism; at the performing of the sign of the New Covenant. This shows how important it is to God that we see and understand the importance of having God's Name called upon His people.

Chapter Fifteen

THE ULTIMATE NAME IN THE END

Philippians 2:5-11- Have this attitude in yourselves which was also in Christ Jesus, who, although He existed in the form of God, did not regard equality with God a thing to be grasped, but emptied Himself, taking the form of a bond-servant, and being made in the likeness of men. Being found in appearance as a man, He humbled Himself by becoming obedient to the point of death, even death on a cross. For this reason also, God highly exalted Him, and bestowed on Him the name which is above every name, so that at the name of Jesus every knee will bow, of those who are in heaven and on earth and under the earth and that every tongue will confess that Jesus Christ is Lord, to the glory of God the Father.

In exhorting us to have humility in relating to one another, Paul cites the example of our Lord Jesus Christ, who showed a tremendous attitude of humility and service, when although He was God, He emptied Himself, and became a human bond servant. (I could write another chapter on the question: Of what did He empty Himself? But that's a separate question, often referred to as the Kenotic Theory, which I will have to save for another time). Then He humbled Himself further to die on the cross, taking all of our sin upon Himself, that we could receive forgiveness for our sins, and have God Himself

INVOKE!

dwell in us. God highly exalted Christ, and gave Him the name that is above all names.

This is a very significant end time event when all people, angels and demons will have to acknowledge God. A literal translation of Philippians 2:11 can give a slightly different picture of what everyone will say in the end when they bow the knee to Jesus. When the Greek verb for confess is used in combination with a short Greek word – "hoti" – it can refer to a direct quote.

By looking at a different passage of Scripture from John 1:20, that cites John the Baptist, we can see the picture. Priests and Levites were sent by the ruling Jews to ask John the Baptist who he was. He didn't want them to confuse him with the coming Messiah, so he was very specific with them.

John 1:20 – And he confessed and did not deny, but confessed, "I am not the Christ." (literal Greek - and he confessed and not denied, and he confessed —- I not am the Christ).

Philippians 2:11 – and that every tongue will confess that Jesus Christ is Lord, to the glory of God the Father. (literal Greek – and every tongue should confess **that** Lord Jesus Christ).

When the end of time comes, and everyone in heaven, on earth, and under the earth bows their knee and confesses, they will say, "Lord Jesus Christ."

The same Greek verb "confess" is used in both of these passages, followed by the Greek word "hoti." In John 1:20

THE ULTIMATE NAME IN THE END

hoti is seen as meaning the following is a direct quote. But in Philippians 2:11 hoti is translated as the word "**that**," instead of signifying the following is a direct quote.

What if we translate it in Philippians 2:11, to mean the following is a direct quote? In verse 11, in referring to the name the Greek literally says, "Lord Jesus Christ." It could be translated this way: "that every tongue will confess, 'Lord Jesus Christ.'" I believe that when the end of time comes, and everyone in heaven, on earth, and under the earth bows their knee and confesses, they will say, "Lord Jesus Christ." They won't be looking at each other saying, "Jesus Christ is Lord." They will be addressing Him directly: "Lord Jesus Christ." That is God's name in the New Covenant, and it expresses our God: three in one, yet one in three, Father, Son and Holy Spirit – the Lord Jesus Christ.

Chapter Sixteen

NO JESUS!

I felt ashamed and embarrassed – not before other people, but before my Lord and Savior, Jesus.

I have been a pastor for about 40 years, and during the last 20 years I've had a rather unique hobby – as a licensed guinea pig judge! Several years ago, I was in southern California judging a weekend show. As part of the festivities, the sponsoring club was having a Friday night banquet. Now many of the guinea pig exhibitors knew that I was an ordained pastor, and I had been asked to give the invocation for the banquet. I had flown in Friday afternoon, and was being hosted in one of the exhibitor's homes. He was very hospitable in getting me settled. During the afternoon he talked with me, and asked that the invocation not be offensive to people, but have a generic tone. Over the years I had come to understand that something as simple as the words of a prayer could be judgmental and offensive, or open and redemptive, so I had no problem agreeing to his request. I also knew that my host's partner was a practicing Jew, so the request did not seem unusual to me. When we had gathered at the restaurant for the banquet, I was seated at a table with several of the exhibitors, including a teenage girl. She and I had a lively conversation about her guinea pigs and the success of her breeding program. I have always been a supporter of young people, so I really enjoyed our interaction. Since we hadn't started yet, and the room was full of people, it was quite noisy. Just before the start of the formal activities, my host came over to where I was seated, and crouched down beside me, to be heard. He let me know that we were about to begin. Just before he got up, he got closer, looked me in the eyes, and said, "Remember, no Jesus!" It was a startling moment, and caught me by surprise. I won't say that his gaze was hateful, but it was very intense, along with his tone of voice. He then got up and left. The teen girl beside me had seen and heard the interaction, and asked me, "What was that about?" I mumbled something about being careful to have a non-offensive prayer.

> **Just before he got up, he got closer, looked me in the eyes, and said, "Remember, no Jesus!"**

I was then called upon to pray. I gave thanks and prayed for God's blessing. I remember using the terms, "God," "Lord," "Father," and "Father God," but did not use "Jesus" in the prayer.

It was the first and only time in my life that I had not used the name of the Lord Jesus Christ in an invocation. After all, I knew that any invocation was to be the calling of God's name over the activity. At that moment, through the evening, and for several days, I felt embarrassed and ashamed. After all, the Bible does say, *"But whoever denies Me before men, I will also deny him before My Father who is in heaven."* (Matthew 10:33).

NO JESUS!

When I failed to invoke the name of Jesus in the prayer, was I denying His name? Was I ashamed of Jesus? *I* felt condemned, along with the shame, but finally realized that Satan was the one condemning me, not God. As I talked with Jesus in prayer, I let Him know that I felt badly about the "nameless" invocation, but that I loved Him and realized that I was not denying my Lord.

I share this to let the reader know that God does not intend to legalistically hold us accountable to invoking God's full formal name every time we pray, or eat, or breathe. Legalism is a human disease that thankfully, God does not have. There are times in life when we cry out, "Lord," or "Father," or "Savior," or "Abba (Daddy)." We may actually have a long conversation with Him, and not mention "Lord" or "Jesus" or "Christ" even once. That won't matter to God; He will just love having the conversation. We know who we mean and He knows who He is, so He responds in loving form to us, even if we haven't used the exact phrase, "Lord Jesus Christ!"

Chapter Seventeen

WHEN WAS THE NAME INVOKED?

When the name of God is invoked He chooses to release His volitional power. He chooses to swing into action when His name has been invoked. What is the principle? **For the sake of His name, God will swing into action!**

"Yahweh bless you, and keep you; Yahweh make His face shine on you, and be gracious to you; Yahweh lift up His countenance on you, and give you peace." The mention of "Yahweh" three times foreshadows the concept of the Trinity, and is a good example of Old Testament type and shadow. The priestly blessing from Numbers chapter 6:24-26 was given to the Israelites with the intent that Aaron and his sons would speak the blessing over the sons of Israel. The invoking of God's name over the people is clearly established as part and parcel of the priestly blessing. Please note that the invoking of God's name was not separated from the pronouncing of His blessing. Scripture does not specify how often this priestly blessing was to be pronounced, but certainly it was given several times during the year at the celebrated feasts, and we know that from the time of Solomon's temple on, it was expressed more and more.

Since the time that the Temple was destroyed the blessing has been expressed at weekly gatherings, as well as special events. Even more so, calling God's Name as part of prayers and blessings, even though it was not the specific priestly blessing of Numbers chapter six, has been practiced by Jewish people for hundreds of years. At the time of Christ, it was pronounced daily in the temple.

For Christians the name of the Lord Jesus Christ was called at the beginning of each new believer's life when they were baptized in water. Through the ages, first with the Roman Catholic Church, and then through the rest of the denominations the invoking of God's Name and pronouncing of God's blessing was practiced at special events, as well as weekly services.

> **It was a separating of the invoking of God's Name from the pronouncing of God's blessing.**

An interesting dichotomy began to appear, and for some reason it has continued on, into the present. It was a separating of the invoking of God's Name from the pronouncing of God's blessing. We see it in two words: Invocation (calling of the Name) and Benediction (giving the blessing). If you ask people what they think those two words mean, they usually say that the Invocation is the prayer offered at the beginning of an event or service, and the Benediction is the prayer offered at the end of the event or service. I don't know why this separation occurred, and I prefer the invoking and blessing being intertwined together, as it is expressed in the priestly blessing from Numbers chapter six.

So the invoking of God's name over a person, place or event, happened frequently and sincerely. That's how we should approach the practice: with sincerity and deep appreciation for how important God's name is, we should invoke the name of the Lord Jesus Christ often!

Chapter Eighteen

WHEN SHOULD WE INVOKE THE NAME?

So when should we invoke the name of the Lord Jesus Christ? Let's ask two other questions that may help us answer the first one. Why should we invoke the name of the Lord Jesus Christ? Invoking the name of God releases His volitional power. God chooses to swing into action when His name has been invoked. **For the sake of His name, God will swing into action!** When do you want God to swing into action? Once a year? Every other month? Weekly? On special occasions? Or more often than that?

When I perform a wedding ceremony, the words of the ceremony may differ somewhat from wedding to wedding. But I always call the name of the Lord Jesus Christ over the couple at least twice: in the prayer of blessing and in the pronouncement. "I now pronounce you husband and wife, in the name of the Father and the Son and the Holy Spirit, the Lord Jesus Christ. What therefore God has joined together, let no man put asunder."

When I baptize someone in water I call the name of the Lord Jesus Christ over the baptismal candidate like this: "Because you have confessed your faith in Jesus Christ, I now baptize you in the name of the Father and the Son and the Holy Spirit – the Lord Jesus Christ."

When I preside over a Child Dedication, as I pray for the parents, I ask for God's blessing and help, and invoke the name of the Lord Jesus Christ over the whole family.

John 14:13, 14 – Whatever you ask in My name, that will I do, so that the Father may be glorified in the Son. If you ask Me anything in My name, I will do it."

John 15:23 – Truly, truly, I say to you, if you ask the Father for anything in My name, He will give it to you. Until now you have asked for nothing in My name; ask and you will receive, so that your joy made be made full.

Matthew 18:19, 20 – Again I say to you, that if two of you agree on earth about anything that they may ask, it shall be done for them by My Father who is in heaven. For where two or three have gathered together in My name, I am there in their midst."

I believe there is wonder working power in His name, and I believe that He wants to swing into action on my behalf.

In church services my wife and I are available to pray for people at the conclusion of services, and many have come with many different prayer requests. We identify with them and agree together in prayer, bringing our requests to God. I always ask in the name of the Lord Jesus Christ, invoking His name over the circumstance and expecting Him to swing into

WHEN SHOULD WE INVOKE THE NAME?

action on our behalf. When I am praying privately and bringing my requests to God, I always ask in the name of the Lord Jesus Christ, invoking His name over the circumstances of my life and expecting Him to swing into action on my behalf. I believe there is wonder working power in His name, and I believe that He wants to swing into action on my behalf. His heart is so full of love and grace that He wants to swing into action on your behalf too!

I am not interested in finding exact rules for timing, or finding some rigid way that prayer must be offered. I am not trying to lay down some new "magical" formula, or secret, hidden, mystical way of saying things. I am not saying that unless you do it in these exact ways, you won't get God's help. I am not saying that we can control God by invoking His name, and He will have to do something for us.

But I have decided that I want all that God wants to give me in this abundant life in Christ. I do believe that invoking the name of God releases His volitional power. When I invoke His name, my personal faith increases, soaring higher and higher. I do believe that God chooses to swing into action when His name has been invoked. I do believe in this principle: **For the sake of His name, God will swing into action!**

Chapter Nineteen

HALLELUJAH

We need to be aware of the power in God's name, and move into our position as children of His name. But it seems like we have been inoculated into God's name being ignored, or reduced to a level of insignificance.

Take a frequent expression of praise we use in our prayers and songs. The word is hallelujah. We use the term many times in each church service, to praise God. It is good that we praise Him, but what does the word actually mean? Does it have anything to do with His name?

I asked a number of people the following question, in order to gather perspective on what people think the word "hallelujah" means:

> 'When you are praying, praising or singing,
> and you use the word "Hallelujah," what does it mean?'

INVOKE!

'When you are praying, praising or singing, and you use the word "Hallelujah," what does it mean?'

"Praise Jesus"

"Praise to the Lord"

"Save me! From whatever I need saving from . . . every day."

From a 9 year old:
"Um, it means you're happy?"

Expressing intense personal joy

Expression of praise, almost like the word "woohoo" is an expression of happiness

"Praise God!"

From an 11 year old:
"Praise the Lord! Praise Jesus!"

All the stuff You (God) did for me and all the stuff You said about me is true.

Loving Jesus

"Praise the Lord."

From the United Kingdom:
"An expression of joy and praise.
It's a deeper power word that allows you to almost explode your praise to the highest heaven."

Gratitude – "Thank you Jesus."
"Thank you Lord." "I praise You." "I thank You."

HALLELUJAH

> The essence of joy because of what God's
> done for me, because of God's love for me.
> God has always been there, past, present
> and future, to lead me to do what
> He designed me to do, and that brings joy.
>
> And another from England:
> It means celebration; overcoming hardship
> and rejoicing. It is something very positive
> and new; something new is beginning.
> We have come through.

An interesting range of responses, isn't it? From the concept of praising and thanking God, all the way to expressing our positive emotions over something that makes us happy; from God-centered all the way to self-centered. These are several good concepts of our attitude toward God, but not really what the term "hallelujah" means.

Hallelujah is an exclamation of worship and a call to praise. The word occurs in the books of Psalms and Revelation. In Psalms it is used in the context of describing the character and conduct of God; what He does for all mankind; what He does to the wicked; what He does for His people. In Revelation 19 it is used in the context of acknowledging the glory, power and saving grace of our God, as well as describing the destruction of the great harlot and God's victory in judging her. It is a transliteration of two Hebrew words: 'Hallel" is in the imperative (command) form, and it commands all who are hearing this to praise; and "Jah" is a contraction of Yahweh, telling all whom they are to praise. When hallelujah is spoken, those who hear are commanded to give praise, not just to any old god, but to the timeless and eternal God, with His formal name being spoken over all who hear. The best definition for

INVOKE!

hallelujah is this: Everyone who hears this (including the one speaking) is commanded to give praise to God.

Back in the 1970's in the charismatic movement, we sang hundreds of choruses, exactly quoting Scripture. I really loved those Scripture songs . . . we were memorizing God's Word as we had fun singing. One song I recall was "Sing Unto God." The lyrics from Psalm 68:4 (KJV):

> Sing unto God, sing praises to His name;
> Sing unto God, sing praises to His name.
> Extol Him that rideth upon the heavens by His name,
> Extol Him that rideth upon the heavens by His name;
> Extol Him that rideth upon the heavens by His name.
> By His name Yah!
> And rejoice before Him and rejoice before Him, and rejoice, rejoice before Him.
> And rejoice before Him and rejoice before Him, and rejoice, rejoice before Him.

Way back then I never understood what "Yah" meant. But I loved singing that song.

The best definition for hallelujah:
Everyone who hears this (including the one speaking)
is commanded to give praise to the Lord Jesus Christ!

You see, every time we speak the word hallelujah, we are saying, "Praise be unto . . . Yahweh!" "Everyone who hears this word is commanded to praise Yahweh." It's no accident that the praise is addressed to God with the speaking of His formal name. Christians around the world use the word, in many different languages, and it is understood as a high expression of praise. Through the ages and in many different languages, it has not been translated, but instead "transliterated," which means it is brought into the next language still being pronounced almost identical to the Hebrew words. But how many people really knew that every time the word is used, God's Name is being called over His people?

Years ago there was a folk song that became very popular: "Michael Row the Boat Ashore." It was actually quite old: an African-American spiritual from the 1800's.

> Michael row the boat ashore, hallelujah.
> Michael row the boat ashore, hallelujah.
> Sister help to trim the sail, hallelujah.
> Sister help to trim the sail, hallelujah.
>
> The river is deep and the river is wide, hallelujah.
> Green pastures on the other side, hallelujah.
>
> Jordan's river is chilly and cold, hallelujah.
> Chills the body but not the soul, hallelujah.
>
> The river is deep and the river is wide, hallelujah.
> Milk and honey on the other side, hallelujah.

The Highwaymen recorded it in 1960, and it became a #1 hit in the US and the UK. Teens throughout America and England sang it again and again. In the chorus and in every verse the word hallelujah was sung twice. Do you think many of those people knew what the word meant? It became a word to say without any real meaning. To me that kind of happening was making the word insignificant, and thereby making God's name insignificant.

There was a movie made in 1965, starring Burt Lancaster, Lee Remick and Brian Keith, called "The Hallelujah Trail." The plot of the whole movie was the attempt to move a wagon train carrying barrels of whiskey to the miners in Denver, during Old West times. Indians tried to steal it; temperance people tried to destroy it; the cavalry tried to stop it. The idea was that if the men of the town could get enough whiskey to drink, they would be happy. Several times during the film, when men either got drunk, or got close to getting a lot of whiskey, they would exclaim, "Hallelujah." The whole movie was a spoof, and yet it did bring forth the idea that when you got the earthly pleasures you desired it would make you happy, and thus you would proclaim, "Hallelujah." I'm not offended by the movie in the least, but it does show me another example of making God's name insignificant.

Through the 20th century, a word with so much powerful meaning about God's name has either come to mean general praise of God, or worse yet, just a general feeling of happiness. That is not the kind of insignificance that we, as Christians, want to accept or practice. The best definition for hallelujah: Everyone who hears this (including the one speaking) is commanded to give praise to the Lord Jesus Christ!

Chapter Twenty

OTHER WAYS WE MAY PRACTICE NAME INSIGNIFICANCE

Generic religion and generic god (do all ways lead to God?)

In these "politically correct" times, we Christians are told to be more tolerant of other religions. People are encouraged to be accepting of other religions and their names. If there is one God, surely He doesn't mind what name humans use to acknowledge Him? I believe the Bible is the inspired, infallible, inerrant Word of God. That means that God breathed it, it does not fail, and does not contain errors.

John 14:6 – Jesus said to him, "I am the way, and the truth, and the life; no one comes to the Father but through Me."

Acts 4:10-12 – let it be known to all of you and to all the people of Israel, that by the name of Jesus Christ the Nazarene, whom you crucified, whom God raised from the dead—by this name this man stands before you in good health. He is the stone which was rejected by you, the builders, but which became the chief cornerstone. And there is salvation in no one else; for there is no other name under heaven that has been given among men by which we must be saved.

I cannot say to people that you can call God Allah, or that Krishna, Buddha or your ancestor's spirit can lead you to God.

As much as it lies within me, I want to be at peace with all people. And I know that God does not want any person to perish, but wants everyone to come to repentance. I honor and respect all people. More than that I want to care for and love all people; so much so that I want everyone to know the truth of salvation in Jesus Christ. I cannot say to people that all ways lead to God, and all religions will turn out right in the end. I cannot say to people that you can call God Allah, or that Krishna, Buddha or your ancestor's spirit can lead you to God. God is not generic and His religion is not generic. If I want people to be saved, then I must share with them that salvation only comes in the name of the Lord Jesus Christ, and they must come to Him and through Him to be saved.

Why do people limit their vocabulary and conversation in such a crude way?

OTHER WAYS WE MAY PRACTICE NAME INSIGNIFICANCE

God d—- it all to h—-!

Something else that makes the name of the Lord Jesus Christ insignificant is the habit of swearing. I was raised to believe that saying "God," or "Jesus Christ." as a swear word, was a violation of the commandment, "You shall not take the name of the LORD (Yahweh) your God in vain, for the LORD (Yahweh) will not leave him unpunished who takes His name in vain."

I grew up on a very small rural farm. We lived about 7 miles out of town. The town of about 5,200 population had one elementary school, one junior high school and one high school. Those are the schools I attended and graduated from. Even though my mom made us go to church every Sunday, and I was raised in Sunday School, I was a typical boy, running with and influenced by the rest of the crowd. My friends and I thought it was cool to use swear words. I still remember an incident that occurred when I was 10 years old: my older brother heard me on the school bus, swearing profusely in an attempt to outdo one of my friends. He threatened to tell mom, and that finally shut me up! I also remember getting in with the wrong crowd in high school, and we thought that the more we used foul language, the more "manly" we were. But when I became a man I put away the childish habit of swearing. As I have worked over the last 20 years in the business community, it has amazed me how many adults use foul language and swearing as part of their regular conversation, especially managers. I am talking specifically of the terms "God," "Jesus," or "Christ," being used, along with many other words that you don't want your children even hearing. Why do people limit their vocabulary and conversation in such a crude way? Is that really the way the world is going?

INVOKE!

What I will say is this: when we refer to the Lord, or Jesus, or Jesus Christ, we should always do it with full awareness that it is the name of our God, and deserves our honor and reverence. Practicing anything less than that makes His name insignificant in our understanding and in our life.

Please don't zap me, God!

Is God looking to stomp on us if we have treated His Name with insignificance? Will God zap you if you don't invoke the name exactly right? Those questions are not even worthy of our thinking; our God is full of grace and lovingkindness toward us, and He wants only the best and abundant life for every one of us.

- Lord, please help me!
- Be healed in the name of Jesus!
- Father, help me now!
- Oh God! Please help!

Will God not act with power on our behalf unless we speak the exact Name?

The new covenant name of our Triune God is the Lord Jesus Christ, and we should practice using that name with full awareness and knowledge of the divine volitional power that name brings. That being said, will God not act with power on our behalf unless we speak the exact Name? That can never be true! God knows our hearts, and He will honor our

OTHER WAYS WE MAY PRACTICE NAME INSIGNIFICANCE

prayers, pleas and praises. The thief on the cross beside Jesus did not invoke the name of the Lord Jesus Christ. "Jesus, remember me when you come in Your kingdom." And Jesus responded, "Truly I say to you, today you shall be with me in Paradise." I remember for myself that when I turned my life over to Him, I said, "Lord, I've made a mess of my life. I know you can do a better job than I have done. I turn my life over to you – please help me." And God responded by coming into my heart and directing my life. Neither I nor the thief on the cross used the exact phrase "Lord Jesus Christ." Yet God still responded to us with His full power and salvation.

God is not in the business of punishing us, if we don't use His name in one exact way. But as we gain insight into His Word, we can walk in bold compliance with its instruction; we can act in faith increasing ways. "In the name of the Lord Jesus Christ I pray, I petition, I move." And God will act on my behalf with power!

Chapter Twenty-One

SUBJECTIVE REFLECTIONS

And when I prayed I called the name
of the Lord Jesus Christ over you.

A brother, a nephew, a niece and a grand-nephew. A few years back I attended the funeral of my oldest brother. He was the oldest of 4 brothers, while I was the youngest. He and I had never been close. When I was seven years old, he had just returned from a stint in the Navy, and was not living in our home. He was about to get married, and on the night of his wedding, right after the ceremony, we packed up and moved 165 miles away to a new town and new life. I kid you not; we drove away that very night. At least that's how I remember it. So it was like I had never really known him and now he lived far away. This was in the late 50's, and it seemed like we only visited with him and his family once a year or so. Then I was 18, and I joined the Army. I visited Seattle just before I was inducted, and it was like he just couldn't relate to me being a man and not a little kid. Over the next several years, my wife and I tried to get closer to him. We used to drive out to his place on Sundays, after morning service, and have dinner with him. My heart was to bring him to the Lord, but he always expressed that he had done too many bad things and wasn't good enough to be a Christian. So time went on. A few years later I was pastoring in Seattle, and crossed paths with several of his children (my nephew and two nieces). I was blessed to bring them to the Lord, and had the opportunity to teach and minister into the life of my nephew. He became a rock solid Christian, and I was blessed to input into his life. I had the privilege of performing the wedding ceremony for him, and he and his wife continue serving the Lord to this day. At the funeral that day, my nephew oversaw the funeral and the grave side service, and I learned from him that he had been able to lead my brother (his own father) to the Lord about a year earlier. God is a master planner! Another of my nieces was there to attend her father's funeral, and she had her son with her. He was a very troubled soul (about 20 years old), and I could sense that he needed the Lord. Now see if you can follow me on this. When this grand nephew of mine was a baby, I had conducted the Baby Dedication service for his mother (my niece). I had not seen him since then (no contact for about 20 years). So after the grave side service several of us went to eat at a local restaurant. Afterward we all had a few minutes together in the parking lot, before we all went in our separate directions. I felt emboldened in the Lord and so I spoke briefly with my grand nephew. The conversation was something like this: "I know you are going through some very tough things right now in your life, but you need to know that God is very interested in you and wants to be very involved in your life. You see, I prayed over you when you were a baby and your mother dedicated you to the Lord. And when I prayed I called the name of the Lord Jesus Christ over you. That means God's power

SUBJECTIVE REFLECTIONS

has been with you and is with you now, and He is calling you to Him for some very definite and important things. You are not alone, and what you need to do now is open yourself to Him. I want you to listen to your uncle as you take the trip home tonight. It is no accident that the name of the Lord Jesus Christ was called over you when you were a baby. Will you listen to your uncle?" On the trip back home my nephew was able to share the gospel with his nephew, and he accepted Jesus as his Savior. You see, I believe that invoking the name of God at that Baby Dedication released the volitional power of God over my grand nephew's life. I believe God chose to swing into action when I called the name of the Lord Jesus Christ over my baby grand nephew. For the sake of His name, God swung into action, and two decades later I saw the results.

Chapter Twenty-Two

AND MORE SUBJECTIVE REFLECTIONS

A daughter's wedding. Fifteen years ago I had the privilege of performing the wedding ceremony for my youngest daughter. We traveled to Texas for the ceremony. I remember so well the privilege of being able to walk her down the aisle and give her hand in marriage to a fine Christian young man. "Who gives this woman to be this man's bride?" "Her mother and I." And then I walked onto the platform and conducted the rest of the ceremony. What a blessing and a thrill! The ceremony, even with special music lasted only a few minutes. But I remember several distinct parts.

When it came to the exchanging of rings, both my son-in-law and daughter repeated these words: "With this ring I thee wed, and I pledge to share with you all that I have. In the name of the Father and the Son and the Holy Spirit, the Lord Jesus Christ. Amen." They both were calling God's Name over their commitment to wed and to share all in life.

Following the exchange of rings, I then made the pronouncement: "Thus you mutually promise. Because you have committed yourselves to one another in holy wedlock and have witnessed this before God and man, and because you have pledged your faith to each other by the exchanging of rings, I now pronounce you husband and wife, in the name of the Father and the Son and the Holy Spirit, the Lord Jesus Christ. What therefore God has joined together, let no man put asunder." This pronouncement was addressed to the couple, but stated to all present. It was like giving public notice: "These two are now married, and have God's Name called over their marriage. God is working for them and their marriage, so don't work against them. . . after all, you don't want to be found opposing God, do you?

There is nothing as powerful as the Name of God, and I truly wanted God's volitional power released in their marriage.

After the pronouncement I laid my hand on the couple and prayed a special blessing over their marriage. I concluded, "This I pray in the name of the Father and the Son and the Holy Spirit, the Lord Jesus Christ. Amen." You see, even with all the love, experience and wisdom I put into this prayer over my daughter and son-in-law, I still wanted the seal of God's Name being called. There is nothing as powerful as the Name of God, and I truly wanted God's volitional power released in their marriage. For the sake of His name, I knew God was swinging into action in their marriage and family.

Well fifteen years and three grandchildren later, I rejoice to see their continued solid commitment to Jesus, and the blessing of God in every aspect of their lives.

AND MORE SUBJECTIVE REFLECTIONS

> I did that in obedience to the Lord
> telling me to invoke His name.

A grandson. It has been years since I have been a pastor in a church. My wife and I are faithful members of a great church in Old Town McKinney, Texas, and we love doing whatever we can for God's people and God's church. I had visions of being the senior pastor of a large church, with all my family in the church, but that's not how it turned out. So all my children serve God faithfully in other churches in the Texas area, and we are content in the Lord. We were invited recently to attend the baby dedication for my grandson. One of the pastors from my daughter's church would be officiating, and we would be there to participate and support as parents. I prayerfully considered the approaching baby dedication for my grandson, and asked the Lord if He had anything He wanted me to say, that I should speak and pass on. Before I go on, I will briefly tell you that I believe the gifts of the Holy Spirit are active today, and that God uses prophecy, the word of knowledge, the word of wisdom, etc., to minister to His church today. So this is what the Lord told me: "I want you to invoke My name over him." "Just as I commanded that My name be put upon and called over the children of Israel, you call My name over him, and this is what I promise: Throughout his life I will exercise My volitional power on his behalf, for My name's sake." I always want to be faithful and obedient to share what God gives me to speak, so I let my grandson's parents know that God had given me a word for him on the event of his dedication, and I would share it with them. Since I was not officiating, I didn't know how this would work out. I was not about to jump up and loudly proclaim something: I believe in decency and order in all things. When the time came, the baby, parents, and extended family were invited to come forward. The pastor took the baby and offered a prayer of blessing, and also led the congregation in a prayer over the parents. I listened carefully to both prayers, and I did not hear God's name called over the baby or the parents. So I quietly moved closer and whispered the name of the Lord Jesus Christ in my grandson's ear. And at one point the two grandfathers prayed over him. I spoke the name of the Lord Jesus Christ twice more over him, as we prayed. I did that in obedience to the Lord telling me to invoke His name. Afterward I gave his parents a written copy of the promise that God had given me. I look forward to seeing the hand of God in his life in the coming years. You see I have faith that invoking the name of God releases His volitional power, and I believe by faith that for the sake of His name, God has swung into action on behalf of my grandson. And I think that's awesome!

Have we missed out on something special?

Re-baptized? I had worked as a staff pastor at several churches in various positions: assistant pastor, youth pastor, Minister of Christian Education and Visitation, etc. Along with another Christian brother, I started a new charismatic church in Burien, WA, a suburb of Seattle. During the next two years, the Lord was really teaching me things about church leadership and doctrine that I had not been exposed to

AND MORE SUBJECTIVE REFLECTIONS

in my years at Bible College. One of the special teachings was about the New Covenant Name of God: the Lord Jesus Christ. As I came to believe in this teaching, I felt the Lord wanted me to join myself to another church, close by in West Seattle. So I resigned as Pastor at the church I had started, and joined myself to this new church. My wife and I joined the church with no promises or expectations as to what we might do in ministry, but with assurance in our hearts that we were where God wanted us to be. Now one of the things I noticed is that the leaders of this church practiced calling the New Covenant name of God over everyone who got baptized in water. They baptized in the name of the Father and the Son and the Holy Spirit, the Lord Jesus Christ. I got to thinking about that. When I was baptized in water, I was baptized in the name of the Father and the Son and the Holy Spirit. And while I was in Practical Theology classes at Bible College, I had been baptized 5 more times in the name of the Father and the Son and the Holy Spirit (we students practiced on each other). My wife and I asked ourselves: have we missed out on something special? Had we been baptized correctly? Did we have to be re-baptized? We concluded that we did not have to be re-baptized. Our baptism was just fine and was not incorrect. But we still asked ourselves if there was something special that we might be missing. We found precedent for re-baptism, when we looked at the disciples in Ephesus who had been baptized into the baptism of John the Baptist. When they heard that the person John the Baptist was pointing forward to was Jesus, they were baptized again in the name of the Lord Jesus, and immediately received the Holy Spirit as Paul laid hands on them. They did not negate their baptism by John, but they responded to fuller truth and received fuller, more profound blessings in God. We also wanted to respond to fuller truth about the name of God, and wanted to receive all that we could from God. So we agreed together and were baptized in water again. In that church they would baptize couples together, so as we stood side-by-side, our arms around one another, one of the elders of that church baptized us in the name of the Father and the Son and the Holy Spirit – the Lord Jesus Christ!

I don't believe that everyone has to be re-baptized. So why did we do it? We had come to believe that invoking the name of God releases His volitional power, and that for the sake of His name, He would swing into action in a special way for us, in our lives, in our family and in our ministry. By faith we embraced that, and have walked in increased faith as a result.

Chapter Twenty-Three

BOAST THE NAME!

Psalm 20:7 NASB - Some boasts in chariots and some in horses, but we will boast in the name of the LORD (YHWH), our God.

KJV - Some trust in chariots, and some in horses: but we will remember the name of the LORD our God.

ASV 1901 - Some [trust] in chariots, and some in horses; But we will make mention of the name of Jehovah our God.

I love each of these translations. Combined together, they express the real meaning and action around the name of God in a Christian's life. While people of the world put trust in their own strength, wisdom, armies, etc., God's people need to guard against putting our trust and faith into the things of this earth.

The Old Testament kingdoms and nations orbited around wars and armies, with horses and chariots. Those were the earthly strengths of the time. But God's ways are not man's ways. God warned that the king of Israel should not multiply horses for himself, or cause the people to return to Egypt to multiply horses. He knew the people would be tempted to take their trust and their boast off of Him (Deuteronomy 17:16). God cautioned and encouraged His people that when they would go out to battle against their enemies and would see horses and chariots and people more numerous than them, still to not be afraid of them, for "Yahweh your God is with you" (Deuteronomy 20:1). He further warned His people that a horse is a false hope for victory; nor does it deliver anyone by its great strength (Psalm 33:17); and that while the horse is prepared for the day of battle, "but victory belongs to Yahweh: (Proverbs 21:31).

> **We need to make mention of God's name in a way that boasts about our God and testifies with thankfulness about the things He has done for us.**

We need to make mention of God's name in a way that boasts about our God and testifies with thankfulness about the things He has done for us. It is right that we remember the things God has done for us; it is also right that we are thankful. But thinking these things is not enough. It's kind of like the husband who says to his wife, "Of course I love you. Why do I always have to say it?" We all know that love needs to be spoken, as well as acted out. So we need to speak God's name with confidence and pride in Him. We are boasting, but not in ourselves or our efforts and armies. We're calling God's name boastfully because we have the greatest God, the best God, the only God!

David – I Samuel 17:38-47 - *Then Saul clothed David with his garments and put a bronze helmet on his head, and he clothed him with armor. . . So David said to Saul, I cannot go with these, for I have not tested them." And David took them off. . . . And the Philistine cursed David by his gods. . . Then David said to the*

BOAST THE NAME!

*Philistine, "You come to me with a sword, a spear, and a javelin, but I come to you in **the name of the LORD** of hosts, the God of the armies of Israel, whom you have taunted. This day **the LORD** will deliver you up into my hands, and I will strike you down and remove your head from you. . . that all this assembly may know that **the LORD** does not deliver by sword or by spear; for the battle is **the LORD's** and He will give you into our hands.*

David acknowledged that man's armor was not going to work for him, and that everyone (especially the armies of Israel) needed to know that deliverance did not come by sword or spear, but by the name of the Lord of hosts! That is why he invoked God's name.

Peter – Acts 3:4-6 - *But Peter, along with John, fixed his gaze on him and said, "Look at us!" And he began to give them his attention, expecting to receive something from them. But Peter said, "I do not possess silver and gold, but what I do have I give to you: In **the name of Jesus Christ the Nazarene** - walk!"*

Peter knew that this man's deliverance was not going to come with silver and gold, even though money is what the man expected. Peter acknowledged that he did not have silver or gold, but, . . . he did possess the power of Jesus Christ. That's why he invoked the name of God!

Those who make God and His name their praise, may make God and His name their trust. As we proclaim His name over people, places and events, our increased faith will lead us into success and victory.

"Lord, I invoke Your name over every event and circumstance of my life, and the lives of others. When I call Your name I will call it boastfully, boldly and clearly. As I call Your name I will be remembering everything you have done for me, with thankfulness and with pride in You! In the name of the Lord Jesus Christ!"

IN CLOSING

Bible traditions with regard to the name of God are important for us to know and use. The Israelites had God's name called over them regularly by their priests. God identified His people as the ones that had His name put upon them, and they were to seriously pray and repent, as needed, to bring His blessings. And His people appealed to His commitment to honoring His own name and the people who had His name put upon them. Sadly God's people did not serve and honor Him as they were supposed to. They presumed He would protect them, regardless of their disobedience. And they failed to see that if they had walked in His ways and paths, the peoples and nations around them could and would have become followers of Yahweh. Over the years they became obsessed with honoring God's name in such a way that they wouldn't pronounce it or practice the commandments of their Law to call it and put it upon their people, their events and their lives. As the New Covenant came into being through the death of our Lord Jesus Christ on the cross, the practice of invoking the name of God continued. We see that the Lord Jesus Christ, the great "I Am," was given the Father's name, and that the New Testament church practiced putting the name of the Lord Jesus Christ on new Christians in water baptism. In our days and times we need to invoke God's name over our people, places and events to increase our faith in His enabling power.

INVOKE!

Invoke! I believe that there is wonder working power in the Name of God. God wants His name put upon and called over His people. He is committed to unleashing His volitional power on behalf of His people and over every situation in their lives, as they take His name and call His name. In Old Covenant times He identified His formal name as "Yahweh," (the Tetragrammaton) because He wants us to focus upon His timeless and eternal existence. In the New Covenant, Jesus Christ identified Himself as "Yahweh," when He said, "Before Abraham was, I am." Jesus Christ is our timeless and eternal God. We see in the New Covenant that the formal name of God is the Lord Jesus Christ, and the timeless, eternal existence of God in the Father, Son and Holy Spirit is expressed in that name. I believe that as we exercise the practice of calling the name of the Lord Jesus Christ over everything in our lives, our faith will increase, and we will see the miraculous, transforming power of God more and more. Let the invoking of the name of the Lord Jesus Christ be our expression of faith in God's supernatural power on our behalf. Christians: honor your God and increase your faith. Invoke!

ABOUT THE AUTHOR

Reed Tibbetts has served for over twenty-three years as an ordained pastor and teacher, and is currently serving as one of the elders of VLife Church in McKinney, Texas, where he ministers as a prophet and teacher.

An honored and decorated disabled veteran of the Vietnam War, Reed is a graduate of Northwest University of the Assemblies of God. Over the many years he has pursued the goal of handling accurately the word of truth, and has developed a reputation as a guardian of apostolic doctrine (the teachings of the apostles).

Through the years Reed has written and printed many teaching notebooks in the churches he has served, but only recently has he turned to the writing and publishing of books for the greater body of Christ.

Reed lives in Princeton, Texas with his wife of forty-five years. They have three adult children and three grandchildren, all of whom are faithfully serving the Lord in their respective local churches.

AUTHOR CONTACT

If you would like to contact Reed, find out more information, purchase books, or request him to speak, please contact:

Reed D. Tibbetts
yahovah3@gmail.com
214-724-7541

www.ingramcontent.com/pod-product-compliance
Lightning Source LLC
Chambersburg PA
CBHW060844050426
42453CB00008B/818